The Battlefield Guide

The Battlefield Guide

HARPERS FERRY
ANTIETAM
GETTYSBURG

poems

Rodger Martin

illustrations by

Chad Gowey

HOBBLEBUSH BOOKS
Brookline, New Hampshire

Composed in Adobe Caslon Pro
at Hobblebush Books

Cover art and illustrations by Chad Gowey

Printed in the United States of America

ISBN: 978-0-9801672-4-5
Library of Congress Control Number: 2009939105

Published by:

HOBBLEBUSH BOOKS
17-A Old Milford Road
Brookline, New Hampshire 03033
www.hobblebush.com

CONTENTS

ACKNOWLEDGMENTS

With deepest respect and gratitude, I acknowledge those who have contributed the support I needed in this lengthy literary journey that has been *The Battlefield Guide*. They include my road trip companions Russell Hay, historian Dean Shultz, the National Park Service rangers, and Marieke, my daughter, who good-naturedly tolerated my idiosyncrasies on so many of these trips and provided the much-needed perspective only youth can provide. Next come my editors and fellow companions in pursuit of language, poets John Hodgen, Linda Warren and Stuart Peterfreund, writer and scholar Gene McCarthy, and the Del Rossi's poetry workshop.

It has been a joy to have crossed genres and collaborate with fellow artist Chad Gowey, whose career as artist and illustrator, is just beginning to take off; and musician/composer Tim Mowry, musicians Val Blachly and Ellen Carlson who crafted the extraordinary music that melds seamlessly with the poetry.

Finally, I need to acknowledge the publishers of the previous editions and the present edition of this book, Dan Lewis and Sidney Hall Jr., artists of the book who care so deeply and movingly about the page they make the book itself a work of art.

INTRODUCTION

*T*he *Battlefield Guide* follows in the footsteps of Herman Melville's *Battle Pieces* and Stephen Vincent Benet's *John Brown's Body*, but rather than use the poems as a viewmaster from which to imagine the Civil War, this volume strives to use those landscapes as a prism from which to view ourselves, Americans, in all the contemporary shades and colors that have evolved since the Civil War.

This fifth edition of *The Battlefield Guide* includes a major addition with the poem "Harpers Ferry." Though the last written, it now initiates the collection. When, in the late 1990s, at Harpers Ferry National Park, I first noticed the monument sponsored by the Daughters of the Confederacy, I sensed only poetry could navigate the emotional and psychological wilderness that we as a people attribute to the events of those years. Since then, the attempt to find a form for Harpers Ferry with which to begin the collection led from one blind alley to another. By 2005, I had put the poem away, unable to discover what would tie it with Antietam and Gettysburg.

In 2009 something changed and I sensed it was time to try again. In the spring, poet John Hodgen and I took a road trip to the battlefields. We were at Gettysburg, when preservationist Dean Shultz showed us the ruins of a mill that had been a stop on the Underground Railway and, a day later, as John and I stopped to throw a few pitches at a lovely ball field just beyond the farmhouse John Brown used to train his believers, the connections began to fall into place. As I reflect on why then and not before, I can't escape the feeling the inauguration of 2009 opened a portal—turned faith to belief that despite all the disastrous decisions we as a people make, we still can come together, build a baseball field for our children, reinvent ourselves, and try again. Literally the entire Harpers Ferry poem came together in May and June with a final quick trip in July with my daughter to fill in the missing introductory six lines.

The other poems began with a trip to Gettysburg in the mid-1990s to investigate whether the memories of youthful explorations to Gettysburg (I grew up nearby) were as real as I recalled or had been exaggerated in my imagination. I expected there would be a 15–30 line poem come of it at most. When I discovered that the places I remembered were not figments of imagination or exaggerations, but simply changes hidden by thirty years of growth, the torrent of language this unleashed caught me off-guard. Then came Antietam, as much a vehicle to examine post 9-11 behavior and an invasion of Iraq based on fraud and propaganda as it was the 1862 battle. By 2003 it became clear, the most dangerous people on the planet are ourselves.

The poems are arranged chronologically in time and geographically from south to north.

With exception of the initials of Henry Clay Powell, whose hand-carved initials I misread through the glass of the old national museum at Gettysburg as *A. C. H.* and from which I created the fictional character Absalom Christian Hart, all historical references are accurate. Endnotes have been added for the curious. I hope the notes are simply that—something, after a poem has been heard and sensed, for the still inquisitive listener to play with later.

One might look at this collection as a literary scavenger hunt for the Civil War buff; indeed, the often overlooked places referenced here are an attempt to reduce the scale of battle from mythic IMAX to the much more personal size of the soldier. For soldiers, a battlefield is about the few square feet surrounding them, square feet in which they desperately try to survive and, whether that fight takes place at Fox's Gap or Crampton Gap, or The Lost Avenue and cavalry fields at Gettysburg, or The Bloody Lane at Antietam, or Prek Klok in Vietnam or a field in Iraq or a ridge in Afghanistan, each is equally intense and equally deadly for the soldiers involved. For a soldier there is no such thing as The Battle of Gettysburg, there is only the amoral chaos of his or her individual and frail attempt to survive.

To stand on these places is to recognize there but for the grace of God and time, could be you or I.

Rodger Martin
August 2, 2009

The Battlefield Guide

Harpers Ferry

THE TOWN

Striated slate foundations squeeze themselves flat
like pages of a national Bible—the book,
layer upon layer locked in shale stacked from shoal
to ridgetop, is the story of ourselves lit by the fire
of gas lamps and determined by the push of the waters,
as much needed, to tame a continent, as desire.

THE POTOMAC

In our seasons of amorous bathing, Venus will loosen
her blouse; but during implacable years, it's Mars,
jock, who pulls tight the straps of his cod. So, chart
the offspring—whether cupid or yeoman archer—the river's still   10
an arrow drawn across the bow of the Blue Ridge,
plucked at the drawstring of the Alleghenies.
Patriot always, the arrow aims at the heart.

Before this border became the great divide,
in the dry days, the dog days, when the river's
sweet waters swung low and like a murmuring
kiss brought the color-blind dark of night,
the river parted for the wheels of the underground
railway sending its children north to hide
among the rocky creeks of tributaries—   20

places with founders names like Penn's Manor
of the Masque[1] where a boy, a ten-year-old's thrill,
could find bundles of food left at dawn
like manna, care packages wordlessly dropped
on his porch, and deliver them to stark faces
waiting beneath the dregs of McAllister's Mill,
Gettysburg, Pennsylvania, 1854.[2]

THE SHENANDOAH

History's tuning fork, river song,
ripple of boyhood imagination,
bridal reins of Virginia,   30
guiding the great sandstone neck
of Massanutten, workhorse of the valley,
and its armies, north, always north.
After midnight, through the mist
that rises from the gurgling waters
about Luray, lightning bugs flicker
like fairies or the souls of cadets
left on the fields of Winchester,
New Market, Cross Keys,
more, more, more. . . . The changeless   40
mist lifts one hundred years
later and two teenage brothers
sleep on blankets in a field
under a sliver of moon, awakened
by the quiet munching of the Holsteins
surrounding them, just enough light
to bring alive only the white
in their coats: each cow a pair
of faint ghosts or The Klan gathering
its sheets to turn back the clock.   50

THE KENNEDY FARM HOUSE,[3] 1859

Amerigho, Amerrique, a Mexica:[4]
A golden spirit's perpetual breath
whirling up and down the continental shelf
becoming a funnel cloud of blood, a gatling gun
of names spit round and round again.

Here, behind logs split and whitewashed,
chinked into the humid Maryland heat,
eighteen men boxed like cartridges
into the attic rooms. Fields here
all slope toward subsistence   60
and if one cannot grow wheat,
one can grow angry.
Add the gravity of morality
and the bile rolls downhill
to the river where it all splatters
against the fire house at Harpers Ferry.
A century and a half later,
under the cold light of a Texas barracks,
when things go wrong—that one forgets
where one hides his wallet. It is still easy   70
to blame a spic, black even better,
than admit stupidity.

THE MONUMENTS[5]

Whether delusion or mid-Depression despair,
the grand-daughters of plantations curtsied
before the chancel of memory, eighth ring
of national hell, and, in defense of the peculiar
carved in stone the death of Hayward Sheperd:[6]
black man, baggage master, protector of trestle,
mouldered by John Brown as their first martyr.

Ten miles north and three years after,   80
in the last green of summer, on the seventh level,
at Fox's Gap,[7] another marker stone
where fifty-eight North Carolinians met
their makers—Enfields[8] of the North. The men
lay juicy in their decomposition, smell
fitting and proper, so their enemies

soberly inebriated dumped them down
a well. Why should anything be pure?
Let us forget again, come back, and stroll
the beauty of the lane there just below limbo,   90
and at its end visit the barbed wire
surrounding the ballistic missile silo,
its hard-on zipped and pulsed for opportunity.

THE ARSENAL

Today, tourists load onto busses, spiral down
like raptors into the dank of this chasm—
coal, water, mortar, rock—hypnotic vortex
mesmerizing backward in time to the gathering
of righteous militia, the burn agains, and generals
who razed cities to save them. Visitors and phantoms
perch wingtip to wingtip on the slate crags and eye   100
the tunnel that belches fire and an iron horse.
The perchers gaze up to a ghostly image in the clouds,
colossus astride the inferno (*Master* Brown to you,
white boy!), the eagle who triangulates
every reconstructed alley, every monument
worth salt. Oh taloned zealot, artist
of the Plutonian trapeze, alighting so nimbly
even Walden's walker stumbled into line;
mouthed so sincerely even the reverend hands
of Dickinson's mentor[9] placed themselves softly   110
in your pockets. Would have seduced Emily herself
had she not wisdom enough to stay out of the world.
Good and evil—Siamese twins—when brazed
like C Street[10] and steel, corrodes itself. Harpers Ferry,
military milliner, magnet for the engineer
with perfect designs for killing. Pastor Brown,
preach us murder, teach us Kansas decapitation,
bleach us in your trinity: father, son and holy ghost
manufacturer of washing machines for blood.

CRAMPTON'S GAP

Aqueduct for words, aquifer of letters: 120
Red sandstone monument to war correspondents.
Townsend's Folly,[11] *Words, words, words,*[12]
filters which embedded reporters distill
for dispatches leaking from the front.
Every town thirsts for its high water mark.
In this pass, in the middle of a history,
at the center of a country that begins
and ends with itself, Athenians from Georgia
died. Four-score-plus later, not too far
for time and crow to fly, the boys of Bedford,   130
Virginia, lay crumpled like soaked cigars,
in the cobbled sands of Normandy.
And in the beginning, *the shot*
heard round the world.[13] More cigars
inked in stone. *Words, words, words—*
sometimes a miracle worker on the page,
sometimes an evangelist parading the stage.
The scribe like *the hand that mocked*
them[14] spins the wheel of syllables and bets
the rolling ball falls right, clarifies   140
the claim: Blood can be turned to water.

TURNER'S GAP

1827

Our elders hoofed this ridge in the arc
of the state—the frying pan before the fire.
Fathers piled rocks above the dolomite
and built a great, stone bottle,
Washington's first monument,[15]
a swiveling Janus peering forward,
backward in time. Chance, that old lover,
always hovering about the edges,
seizes geography, pinwheeling place   150
into the whirling center of its maw.

1862

On a mid-September morning,
butternut patriots looked east
at blue patriots slithering up the slopes,
unraveling until flame forked
from their tongues, singeing gray
into blistered coils that snaked down
the darkening slopes and by next day's morning
blue looked west at gray columns undulating
toward rest on the banks of Antietam.   160

Antietam

THE NORTH WOODS

In that final burst of blossom,
in the clarity of early morning air
even the wasp, its mandibles skewering
aphids from the fleshy cusp of the day
lily drones, "Everyone is alone."

Sometimes friends, if they ramble this world,
begin to puff like gods—so, he and I, our wind
suffocating summer's last swales much as the night
one hundred and forty years before, Hooker's squadrons
on a last sortie, sucked life from two hundred   10
caught between the corn cribs and North Wood.
But robbing cradles hardly scratches that itch,
and we, bloated too, sallowed on wealth, must,
even in early daylight, warble through our jowls
in hope we can re-ambush innocence—or, lacking that,
assault a church. Here, two are safer apart.

THE DUNKER CHURCH

Boots echo on the hardwood;
Stern, straight-backed benches
broach the question directly:
"Who do you think you are?"   20
A polished wooden table sits
beyond the potbelly stove
and waits an answer in writing.

On that man-silent September sunrise
nature still spoke freely to itself;
but, by day's end, even the birds—struck so dumb—
refused to sing, nor would they return next spring.[16]

Square frame, equilateral roof,
eight windows, centered doors,
symmetrical as heaven. It will do.   30

THE WEST WOODS [17]

Sedgwick's division advanced casually,
in three, long, well-dressed lines, no different
than my absent friend who, like them, appears
suddenly on the horizon. Does he know
I have him in my sights, wonder about his thoughts,
know I will wait until I cannot miss?
What proper imaginings for a man
walking toward an end? Time on soul?
That die cast years before like scent
of thatch or limestone's aroma rising on   40
the morning's evaporating mist. My friend
strides purposely toward where I hide,
his reverie embraced in safe silence.
He is closer now. I can see
the folds in his shirt. The distinct blackness
of his shorts. The dark stockings,
the low-cut sneakers. He still does not know
he is in my sights. (Oh, he knows
I am here. Veterans always know.
Soldiers' therapy.)   50
I see his chest rise and fall
with the rhythm of his walk.
I hear the gravel crunch beneath
his sneakers, close—a forlorn hope
somehow he can hit a thousand.
At which step do I interrupt, simply
squeeze the trigger and watch
the entire first wave collapse
like water on a tired beach.

NORTH OF MUMMA'S FARM

They said, before the next volley,   60
when the smoke lifted, the ground writhed
as if in spasm like dark maggots
suddenly exposed to light.
How quickly a mind disconnects,
runs back-and-forth. Rover-red-rover
send someone on over 'til woods
and cornfield exhaust their flesh.

Would Clara Barton come again,
undo the done, pile straw
for mangers, petticoats for bandages,   70
raise my already martyred friend,
cradle him for a drink? But a ball,
angry as vinegar, forbids comfort
to the crucified. It would sear
through her sleeve and bore again
this man from armpit to armpit.[18]
Let the water pour with the blood—
this communion of holes and time.

THE BLOODY LANE

It is still early enough to try again at the front
bank of a sunken road. The first shot   80
opened Colonel Gordon's lower calf.
Certainly blood will make it awkward
to back the honking to Lee, "These men
will stay here until the sun goes down." [19]
A second opened the flesh toward
the knee. His word was at stake.
The third removed the bicep and tendons
of his left arm. He had pledged.
The fourth ball littered its wooden plug
and his clothing in its path through   90
his shoulder. It's time to clump like Ahab
among his Alabama corpses searching
an escape clause. He found a father dying
shuddering from the thud of bullet
after bullet to protect the body of his son.
"'Here we are,' the father whispered
to the god of shell, 'My son is dead,
and,' as if he were tucking the boy to bed,
'I shall go soon, but it is all right.'" [20]

And it is only noon.   100

To the west, Private Robert E. Lee, Jr.,
shuffled, downcast, last gosling in line,
aside Poague's only cannon left.
Robert E. Lee, gander, ordered the gun
back to the front. A gosling cannot help
its petulance, " 'You're not
going to put us in the fight again?'
Lee the father, the general, pointed

his bandaged hand toward Gordon's
sunken road, 'Yes, my son, I need you
to drive those people away.'" [21]

And we still drive away, automobile tires
rolling in soft denial as if—as if—anything
proper, anything Godly could make this right,
as if oil blackening an untouched tundra
could glue the pieces together again.

BURNSIDE'S BRIDGE [22]

Broadway demands a leading man
and an amphitheater suits an historical reprise
so Toombs chose his crags and name well.
The general liked his players: three hundred Georgians,   120
14,000 of the Ninth Corps on Union wages,
who Toombs (having read his lines) knew
would have to walk on water or rush
the stone arches, a stage all his barrels
could spotlight—take a man and make him a star. [23]

Is it better to be Act I: a Connecticut Yankee
on the wrong court trying to make water
four feet deep solid as pavement?
"One if by sea . . ." Every wound
meant drowning. Act I: Those that didn't   130
waded back to land. [24]

Or Act II: "Maryland, my Maryland"
border battle in a border state,
groundlings shooting groundlings
on both sides of the creek? [25]

With character actors from the Granite State,
the Yankee Marylanders formed a column
four-wide, jogged like ducks in a gallery,
along a road parallel to the stream
and tried to waddle the dry way all   140
funneled onto the spotlit stage.
West Point directors worked it out:
Boys nearest the creek become logs,
breastworks in the finest sense,
accepting the wit from Georgia,
protecting the actors' guild jogging aside them.

But the barbs were too sharp, their skins too thin,
and the muzzle velocity too great.
Act II, Scene One: Those left scamper back to the hill.[26]
Act II, Scene Two: They do it all again.   150

Act III: Pennsylvania's turn to raise the curtain,
 add pinch-hit bread-basket heft. The script read:
"to hell with columns" so they rush the bridge,
flailing at balls too fast to hit or see.
Act III: They piled in mounds, a sold-out audience,
behind a stone wall stage right to the bridge.[27]

Act IV, Scene One: The rules of baseball[28] had not
been perfected and one director was
from New York. He rewrote the script:
If I let the corpses bluster (We have more   160
then they.) I can let my New Yorkers swing
and make myself a star.

Empire Builders, even then cynical enough,
sensed not God, Hollywood,
Doubleday, or country can save a fireballer
who has no relief, so first made sure
the Georgians ran short on rifles;
second, demanded two barrels of whiskey,[29]
then—
Act IV, Scene Two: They took the bridge.   170

The general would have liked an encore,
but there was no one left to clap.

It is only one p.m.

HARPERS FERRY ROAD

How giving of war, intermission in mid-afternoon,
opportunity for my friend and I to hop a wall and trudge
through brambles and stubble toward a post-and-rail fence
that permitted a Virginia musician, prone in shallow safety
against the low rise of earth which naturally silts
the base, time to compose on the swell of a minie ball
as it whistled overhead: "E flat to F... receding to D."[30]   180
We try to bluff, "A trumpet player grasping Doppler?
Had he survived, perhaps The South could have had
The Bomb a century sooner—tried it out on Harrisburg."

Not so, you think? If you could have seen us
the wrong saviors of John Brown's body,
like A. P. Hills in red-shirted, late afternoon truck
against the Ninth Corps' flank, see the lines
walk up and the lines fall down,
see Sharpsburg's buildings aflame
against the lowering sun, black smoke   190
billowing across a face so full
with the day's gore it barely balances
itself above the horizon—Oh, had we sat
with Jenkins' cavalry on the west bank
of the Susquehanna in June of the next year,[31]
we would not have wasted The Bomb
on a polluted city farther to the east.

Silence gathers the weight of centuries.
I hear its voice carry in it the chorus
of the children never born. They skip   200
among the cannon, question their jilted parents,
"What did you do in the war? Can we
stroll together through the corn?"

In the corner, outside the walls, two doe nibble
next to the ghost of a tall, powder-stained teenager
who sits numbly at the feet of his grimy, bearded father
a corpse lying on its back.[32]

My friend and I walk back to the church,
sit silent, stare across the wood benches
dividing the empty hall,   210
not daring to speak of the huff,
the puff we hide in our minds,
knowing too well what we are able,
too well the push of the itch,
too well how easy we scratch inside
this church closed like a lily at night.
It will open with dawn, and we hear
the mandibles rasping at the door.   218

Gettysburg

I. VISITORS' CENTER

I am your battlefield guide and your
silence makes it proper to waffle in time.
At parkland like this, late at night, voices
still rise from Earth to question the battlefield poacher,
"Why are you here?" If I, old poacher,
cannot lay my metal detection down
and walk away from my clothes there is nothing
further to say where history's reddish cropping
overlooks the tide-wracked plates scouring this planet
we might as well have named the god of war.   10
Sometimes the strain's so deep I fear
the elastic limit of rock, the snap that will liquify
our fill and slide it all into the sea.
So I scout life's edges and loot a legion's faded
compost for bandage, for salve, for hope. There
survivors peacefully dwindle to none and because
there are no ears to hear sound itself ceases.

Do not tour the field when the sun bakes
the busses like bread or sizzles like egg the family
car or reflects like whitewash off Leister House clapboards,   20
headquarters of the Army of the Potomac.
Once, on a Friday afternoon before
the holiday, its picket fences enclosed
the sliced chunks of a Meade orderly carved
in two by a Whitworth's [33] line. Wait
instead until rain from a muffled sky drips
slowly off the underside of sycamores,
their mottled bark peeling like flesh
sloughing off the bloated carcasses of horse
scattered silent in Leister's lanes, ditches,   30
and fields. Their legs seem poised to gallop across

the low banks of cloud, so parents huddle
their broods into safer stables inside. There
they watch televised history showcase tunics
of re-enactors too clean to know the fine,
machined precision of Springfield lathes [34] turning
metal and inclined planes into sheen of fuse plugs
that smoothly screw their paper packs of powder
into the black, pig-iron casings scored
to crescendo in fragments that suavely take off a jaw   40
leaving the rube tottering, puzzled at what he's seen and lost.

II. CEMETERY RIDGE[35]

Outside, the mist snakes like smoke
across the silence, coiling back upon itself
while the automobile tires hiss
against the wet pavement. A good ear
easily hears a round shot rebound
off a boulder, spin among the troops,
its hot fuse sputtering. Every soldier become
math whiz, calculating the odds,
wondering if or when it will burst.   50

Hancock[36] still struts this avenue with the flourish
of his name. He knew shades and stages
and how the heart bleats to metallic embrace,
a bayonet's pelvic thrust, the critic's curse.
When he grabbed a private from Maine
by both shoulders and planted him
facing the audience charging up the slope,
"Will you stay here?" who could not say yes
to those stars? And the cast formed on his left,
bowing again and again to the applause in pursuit   60
of an Oscar that aches down even the sane.
Give him credit. We all end up in bronze.

III. NAVIGATING THE CAVALRY FIELD[37]

Today we ride with a guide named Custer. She
is master of trail, horse, and narrative. She
understands the other old stallion who loathed other stallions
and would hurl and hurl himself against them,
and his herds follow and follow to avoid the loneliness
that becomes the last to fall. There are seventeen
of us, almost a troop, almost enough
to start the fight again where Rummel's Barn   70
divides the fields between the woods. A Custer
now and then, a Rummel then and Rommel now[38]
like Hector's sword and Achilles' shield, bronze
and iron; the characters, their weapons split by the ages[39]
as if it matters to riders, or listeners, or sages.
We simply follow the masticated scent
of fodder, the lips' prehensile blubber, the clink
of steel, and creak of leather. We follow the swish
of the tail ahead and the steady clop of horseshoe,
a lullaby asleep on the move, always on   80
the flanks missing the bigger show. Until
out of nowhere the crack of lightning
like a shell burst and we all leap to rapture
before our hearts can recatch their beats.

IV. LITTLE ROUND TOP[40]

Before this war, a craftsman named George Leonard
of Keene, New Hampshire, exquisitely milled a target
rifle.[41] Somehow it became a part
of the unexpected clearance, the fire sale
demanding men like Amos Fortune be free.[42]
Leonard's gift worked its way to Georgia   90
and the initials "A. C. H." Such a Georgian
would know his craft like the writer knows ink,
like the flautist knows wind: a song for any occasion—
for turkey, or venison, or mink. Absalom Hart[43]
never crossed the Georgia line but perhaps
he had a son, Absalom Christian Hart,[44]
who needed life beyond Cobb County, Georgia,
and found Penn's Woods good country to go
about his father's business. A bullet to the gut

dropped General Weed[45] from his horse and when Weed   100
tried to whisper, Captain Hazlett bent
to listen. A bullet to Hazlett's brain, a second;
a quick claim to mystify the parliamentarian.
How unseemly for a gentleman to splatter
gray matter on another without opportunity
for apology, a new founders' creed:
Annihilation without representation.
Had there been corporations, such efficiency
would have pleased Generals Electric and Motors,
and Microsoft would cherish the simplicity—   110
on or off, one or zero.

Later, somewhere in the Devil's Den,
a concussion sought out the name behind the initials,
Absalom Christian Hart, old friend,

and separated his life from his rifle's.
One hundred and thirty-seven years later,
we haphazardly travel from Keene, New Hampshire,
look through thick glass at a rifle with patient,
hand-carved initials: one or zero, on or off.

V. THE WHEATFIELD[46]

At last, some evidence of speed beyond light.[47]   120
When concentrated lasers energize a gelatin
just as the lead edge of a lightwave enters
one side of that viscosity like the flag-waving sergeant
draws his troops toward the muzzles' acrid smoke,
instantly the entire wave emerges complete
from the far side of the gel. Let me
make wormholes of gluten. Mount up, ride
the coagulum hard beyond the century, get
ahead, rein in, look back, and see
the long butternut brigades move again and again   130
against blue lines, hammer them back upon
themselves, squeeze them in the clench of their vise.

Blue feet sculpted into weathered blades of tin
and copper, blood mixed with gold turned them
green. They sprouted faster than the South could reap.
Cut us down they said. We are the grass of our Union.
All day the combines labored in dusty smoke
but that night—even a John Deere grows weary—
Longstreet[48] stopped under a maroon sunset dismayed
at the fields yet to cut. Anywhere else   140
in the universe blue would crack, genius prevail,
great theory written, but not here, not
here, where Sickles[49] made wheat and peaches famous.

VI. LOST AVENUE [50]

Behind the developments, in a place no roads reach,
there is an avenue open to chickens, cattle
and ghosts. A lane bounded by two rows
of crude stone walls, a few burled trees.
Here Neill's Brigade skirmished with Virginians
while Pickett made better Virginia news elsewhere.
Even then there were pennies among the silver.   150
Flying eagles made cents before Lincoln.
Today Neill's monuments draw heifers
not tourists—copper in place of nickel plate.

Only fifty fell here—two baseball teams
playing out their schedule. Forty years
ago, my brother and I sought out the old trees,
found the gnarls that might hold fragments or minie balls
and tried to cut them out. Later, beneath
the full moon, we slipped across Rock Creek,
crept to Spangler's Spring where the mist covered   160
the base of the plinths. We heard the granite horses.
Their soldiers began to whisper in the moonlight
as they gathered water for their wounded.
It is better cows visit here each day,
wearing down the path, ruminating the grass.

VII. CULP'S HILL

John Wesley Culp, Gettysburg son gone down
to Winchester, enlisted, came home
invader. He visited first his sister,
then his cousin's farm—family stretched
taut as a tent trying to shelter all   170
from the thunderhead flattened to an anvil
that would hammer a quarter million
into submission: craniums split like melons,
the peculiar thwack and thud of bullet
hitting home. Home? What brought John Wesley?
The memory of toes wrinkling the water of Rock Creek?
The primeval odor of a breakfast cooked
while he slept? Did he wake confused as the dog
from Steuart's Brigade leaping ahead of his master
as they charged the hill, determined to fetch   180
that imaginary ball bouncing in Union lines,
suddenly rocked backward. Puzzled,
one leg shot away, the dog nuzzled gray bodies
for reassurance, a familiar scent;
And there, in the no-man's land between,
riddled from both sides, God's handy companion,
stretched for explanation, licked
a blue soldier's hand and died.
Later, General Kane ordered it buried,
the only Christian on the field.[51]   190

And Wesley Culp, name pup-carved
into his rifle, played ball a few hours longer
by the fishing hole, in McAllister's Woods,
on McAllister's Hill, finally climbed a boulder
to catch a glimpse of Neill's lost brigade
and caught the ball in his forehead.
They left the family his rifle butt
folded like a flag. [52]

McPherson's Ridge rolls in green and columbine,
but already yellow busses drill for their autumn   200
parade. It is every student's dream that their teachers
march off to war. So what did the teachers do
when their prize student, John Reynolds,[54] the pupil
who aced every quiz, never missed an assignment,
rode into the thud of a minie ball
spit from the mouth of a sharpshooter,
a classmate of Absalom Christian Hart,
and, before he could answer a single question,
went down without a word?
The corps' first of The First, a corpse,   210
a single letter, swirl of ink, the difference
between pass and fail. What did the teachers do
over summer vacation when their public,
on the very first day, broke on both flanks
and ran off to the beach? They did
what all good teachers do, stood
shoulder to shoulder near a railroad cut
spread open like the seams of a book,
dropped in droves and died.

IX. SEMINARY RIDGE [55]

I must learn to soften and labor like Traveller,[56]   220
who sensed in that great simpleness of horse
there are some weights worth bearing. I must
balance the seat of a white-bearded man with a drawl,[57]
stooped with diarrhea, heart walls
dissolving, his daughter dead, his wife dying,
his sons exhausting the war's nine lives. I must
carry his burdens out to meet the remnants
and few generals returning from that distant copse
of trees.[58] Three times in three days his men had breached
those shores and found themselves too human for more.   230
What else is left for him to speak but truth,
"It is all my fault." I will carry this man
who understood his state traded wrongs
into Stars and Bars,[59] rednecks and lynching but still
kept and dressed in linen for tea with Ulysses
Grant in the parlor of Wilmer McLean's[60] on an oblate
sphere where the tides begin and the tides end.
I will carry this man just behind my withers,
serve as a beacon, a memory of bird song
cool as water bubbling through green pasture,   240
wind chimes softly burnishing air. I will
carry this man because in the end I have
no choice but to bronze myself to some planet—
bronze myself to a home.   244

Notes

HARPER'S FERRY

1   A land grant the Penn family reserved for itself from a treaty with the Indians of land west of the Susquehanna River, part of which later became York and Adams Counties, Pennsylvania. Gettysburg became the county seat for Adams County.

2   See Bradley Schmehl's painting commissioned by preservationist Dean Shultz based on an event contained in *Episodes of Gettysburg and the Underground Railroad* by J. Howard Wert, edited by G. Craig Caba (Caba Antiques: Gettysburg) 1998.

3   The location where John Brown trained his men for the raid on Harpers Ferry, October 16, 1859.

4   Words springing from three of the theories about the naming of the New World: Amerigo Vespucci, the Carib name for Nicaragua, and the mistranslation of the Spanish "to Mexico."

5   The Hayward Sheperd Monument is located across the street from the railroad station in Harpers Ferry, erected in 1931 by the Daughters of the Confederacy and Sons of Confederate Veterans. The wording "peculiar relationship" when referencing slavery is their own. The North Carolina monument is located in the woods south of the Wise farmhouse at Fox's Gap, South Mountain Battlefields, Maryland.

6   Stephen Oates, *To Purge This Land with Blood.* (Harper & Row: New York) 1970, ch. XIX, 292. Sheperd walked from the station, out the railroad trestle to see what the trouble was about when he was shot by one of John Brown's raiders.

7   Battle of South Mountain, Maryland, September 14, 1862.

8   Enfield rifle muskets (one of the standard issue weapons during the Civil War) were manufactured in the mills along the Connecticut River at Enfield, Connecticut.

9   Oates, 215–216. Thomas Wentworth Higginson, Unitarian minister from Worcester, Massachusetts, is best known for his correspondence with Emily Dickinson. Less well known is his strong backing of John Brown and his Kansas activities. Approval of Brown's work, according to Oates, also came from Thoreau and Emerson (196–197).

10 Jeff Sharlot, "Sex and power inside 'the C Street House,'" the Washington, D.C., home for the fundamentalist Christian group which nicknames itself the Christian Mafia. *Salon.com*, July 21, 2009.

11 In 1884, George Alfred Templeton, wealthy journalist, designed and built a memorial arch for war correspondents of the Civil War on the site of The Crampton's Gap portion of the 1862 South Mountain battles. The property is now part of Gathland State Park in Maryland.

12 William Shakespeare, *Hamlet*, II, ii, 192.

13 Ralph Waldo Emerson, "Concord Hymn," at the dedication of another battle monument, April 19, 1837.

14 Percy Bysshe Shelley, "Ozymandias."

15 In 1827, residents built the first monument to George Washington at the top of South Mountain. Today the Appalachian Trail passes at its feet. General George Braddock's army passed this way on the march to its massacre during the French and Indian War. George and William, cousins of Daniel Boone, settled Boonsboro in 1792.

ANTIETAM

16 Residents of Sharpsburg noted birds did not return to Sharpsburg the following spring. Whether they were killed by bullets and shells just before they migrated south or decided there must be better places to nest one can only speculate.

17 Shelby Foote, *The Civil War: A Narrative, Fort Sumter to Perryville* (Vintage Books: New York) 1986, 688–692. This portion of the field also includes the infamous cornfield, a 40-acre field that changed hands four times and was at the center of the morning battles where three Union corps and three Confederate divisions shattered themselves.

18 John Priest, "O My Strength, Haste Thee To Help Me," *Antietam: The Soldiers' Battle,"* (Oxford Univ. Press: New York) 1989, ch. 11, 175. Clara Barton, founder of The Red Cross, worked at a field hospital just north of the morning's action.

19 Priest, 137, 162, 169–170. Despite these wounds and another to his face, John Gordon survived. He later commanded Lee's Second Corps.

20 The 6th Alabama under Gordon was almost destroyed in this lane.

21 Besides his youngest son, a private, Lee's other son and nephew (Rooney and Fitzhue) became generals.

22 This stone bridge (Rohrbach Bridge) picked up a new name after General Ambrose Burnside of the Union IX Corps, a gregarious general who later commanded The Army of the Potomac at Fredericksburg. It is said his distinctive facial hair coined the word sideburns.

23 Priest, 223. Lt. Col. Eugene Duryea was told by his division commander that he would earn a general's star if his 2nd Maryland soldiers could take the bridge.

24 The first attack was directly across the creek and the bridge.

25 Groundlings refer to the patrons standing at the foot of the stage in Elizabeathean theaters. Maryland units fought for both sides at many battles, but this was the first in their own state. The State of Maryland battle monument stands just north of the Visitors' Center, Antietam National Battlefield Park, Sharpsburg, Maryland.

26 Lyman Jackman of the 6th New Hampshire writes about this second failed assault on the bridge. *Sixth New Hampshire Regiment* (Old Books Publishing: Earlysville, VA 1996) 104–105.

27 These were the soldiers of the 51st and 48th Pennsylvania.

28 Though General Abner Doubleday did not fight at Burnside's Bridge, the man given credit for inventing baseball served as a division commander earlier in the day, fighting with the Union I Corps in the North Woods.

29 Priest, p. 232. Colonel Edward Ferraro was asked by a private if he would give the 51st New York and 51st Pennsylvania their whiskey if they took the bridge. His response: "Yes, by God. You shall have as much as you want, if you take the bridge. I don't mean the whole brigade, but you two regiments shall have just as much as you want . . . if I have to send to New York to get it, and pay for it out of my own purse; that is if I live to see you through it."

30 Priest, 255–256. As told by Alexander Hunter of the 17th Virginia in the afternoon.

31 In late June of 1863, just prior to the Battle of Gettysburg, Jenkins troops viewed Harrisburg across the Susquehanna River and fired artillery at the capitol while Earley's troops reached the river at Wrightsville, Pennsylvania, and looked across at Columbia.

32 Priest, 167.

GETTYSBURG

33 Whitworth refers to a British-made, breech-loading artillery piece used by Confederate artillerymen at Gettysburg. It was noted for its accuracy and range.

34 Springfield refers specifically to the major Union armory located at Springfield, Massachusetts, and in general to all the Union arms manufacturers spread along the Connecticut River Valley. They were noted for their precision work and even as late as World War II, the River Valley machine shops remained a priority target for Nazi bombers if they had reached the continental United States.

35 Cemetery Ridge remained the main Union defense position during the three-day battle.

36 Hancock refers to General Winfield Hancock, commander of The Union II Corps. He took field command of the army after General Reynolds was killed. He was wounded on the third day. The incident refers to the general personally taking command of a Maine regiment and asking it to stand and halt a Confederate breakthrough on the second day. Hancock insisted on wearing a clean, white, very visible shirt to every battle: therefore, the allusion to John Hancock's signature on The Declaration of Independence.

37 The cavalry battlefield is located about three miles to the east (rear) of the main Union army.

38 Rummel, beside referring to the farm directly in the center of the cavalry battle, also puns off German Field Marshall Irwin Rommel of the Second World War, commander of the Afrika Korps. Rommel was famous for his lightning-strike tactics.

39 Hector and Achilles, in spite of being central characters in *The Iliad*, historically appear to be from different ages. Hector is considered a Bronze Age soldier, Achilles an Iron Age soldier. Homer's epic combines both into a single time period.

40 Little Round Top, located at the southern tip of the Army of the Potomac, was one of the lynchpins of the Union defense at Gettysburg.

41 The target rifle existed as an exhibit in the old Visitors' Center at Gettysburg.

42 Amos Fortune was an African-American freeman who owned and operated a blacksmith shop in Jaffrey, New Hampshire, in the late 1700s. His homestead is preserved and serves as the site of an annual summer lecture series.

43 Absolam Hart is listed on the muster rolls of the Sixth Georgia State Line, a militia regiment not to be used outside the state line without permission of the governor. This should not to be confused with the Sixth Georgia Infantry which fought at Devil's Den.

44 The name Absolam Christian Hart is poetic license. This rifle was the first artifact to be exhibited from the battlefield. Shortly after I wrote this poem, a park specialist determined the initials are really H. C. P. and belonged to a Henry Clay Powell of Texas who was wounded at Gettysburg. (Jorgensen, Kathryn. "Owner of 1st Gettysburg Artifact is Identified," *The Civil War Times*, Vol XXIX, No. 8, September 2008, 1.

45 General Weed was a commander in the Union III Corps killed on Little Round Top. Captain Hazlett was an artilleryman.

46 A battlefield located below and to the northwest of Little Round Top.

47 The light-speed reference comes from a 1999 story about an experiment which suggested there may be speeds greater than 186,000 miles per second.

48 Lt. Gen. Peter Longstreet commanded Lee's First Corps. Lee nicknamed him his "Old Warhorse."

49 General Dan Sickles commanded the Union III Corps. There is a monument in The Wheatfield noting where he lost his leg. The amputated leg is now an exhibit in Washington, D.C. One cannot help but think about the monument to Gen. Benedict Arnold's leg at the Battle of Saratoga during the American Revolution.

50 The Lost Avenue exists as a sliver of the National Military Park surrounded by private property. Access can be gained with permission of property owners. It is a ridge located just north of the Baltimore Pike directly south of the Rock Creek bridge. McAllister's Mill, the underground railway stop, was located across the creek.

51 Harry Pfantz, "The Last Attacks," *Gettysburg: Culp's Hill and Cemetery Ridge* (Univ. of North Carolina Press: Chapel Hill) 1993, ch. 17, 319–320.

52 Pfantz, note 2, 465

53 The title refers to a regiment composed mostly of Pennsylvania school teachers who fought on the First Day.

54 General John Reynolds commanded the Union I Corps. He had been offered command of the Army of the Potomac prior to Gettysburg but declined. He was born in Lancaster, Pennsylvania, less than fifty miles from the battlefield, and was killed early on the First Day's fighting.

55 Seminary Ridge was the main Confederate battle line at Gettysburg.

56 Traveller was the name of Robert E. Lee's horse. Its skeleton was preserved at the Virginia Military Institute in the Shenandoah Valley. The remains are now buried near there.

57 The white-bearded man refers to Robert E. Lee, commander of the Army of Northern Virginia (Confederates) from 1862 until the end of the war.

58 The copse of trees was the focal point of Pickett's Charge.

59 Stars and Bars was the nickname of one of the Confederate flags.

60 McLean at the beginning of the Civil War owned a farm near Manassas Junction, Virginia, site of the First and Second Battles of Bull Run. In order to avoid the fighting, he moved to Appomattox Court House, Virginia, and it was in his house that the final battle of the Civil War came to an end with Lee's surrender to Grant. In a metaphorical sense, the war began and ended at his front porch.

ABOUT THE AUTHOR

RODGER MARTIN is a touring artist for the New England Foundation for the Arts (NEFA). He has received an *Appalachia* Award for poetry and a New Hampshire State Council on the Arts award for fiction. He has received fellowships from The National Endowment for the Humanities to study T. S. Eliot and Thomas Hardy at Oxford University and John Milton at Duquesne University. His work has been published in literary journals throughout the United States and China where he also wrote a series of essays on American poetry for *The Yangtze River Journal.* He and six colleagues are the focus of the book *On the Monadnock: New Pastoral Poetry* (Chinese Drama Press: 2006, Bejing). Martin often collaborates with other artists. His Portsmouth Voice and Vision project, *Anthem Concatenus,* with painter Vicki Arico now hangs in the Portsmouth Court House. He is the managing editor of *The Worcester Review* and teaches journalism at Keene State College. As a journalist, he regularly covered Democratic National Conventions between 1976 and 2004. Additionally, Martin directs The Milton Ensemble, dedicated to the dramatic presentation of *Paradise Lost* by John Milton. This is his second collection from Hobblebush Books. *The Blue Moon Series* was released in 2007 and chosen by *Small Press Review* as one of its summer picks.

ABOUT THE ILLUSTRATOR

CHAD GOWEY was born and raised in rural Massachusetts. A graduate of the Rhode Island School of Design (BFA Illustration, 2009), he now works as a professional illustrator in the Boston area. Working in paint, ink, digital media and beyond, Chad is fascinated by everything from the masters to the fantastic. When he's not in the studio, Chad enjoys sailing on Cape Cod, working on the family farm, or daydreaming on the Red Line.